To Steve,

HOF

Gieat man,

Great Friend!

GROWN ASS
LEADERSHIP

How to Be an Accountable Grown Ass Adult in Today's Business World

Brandon Fey

Inspired Press Publisher
1333 Chelsea Court
Morrow, OH 45152
www.inspiredpresspublisher.com
513-256-1792

ISBN: 978-1-7324634-7-9
Library of Congress Control Number: 2019916770

Introduction

I am not perfect. Neither are you. I have screwed up and have learned from every one of my mistakes. This book, then, is not to make me look like the know-all end-all. It is just some simple observation of others, as well as myself, operating in the business landscape. This includes 20-plus years of retail, leadership, managing people, consulting businesses, and overall dealing with people on a daily basis. I'm just like you. My last name doesn't allow me a trust fund or give me a family business set up for me. I get up every day and grind to provide for my family just like 95% of the workforce. At the time I began writing this book, I had $236 in my checking account. But I have a payday coming up, and I will survive. My point is that I'm no millionaire preaching how to make more money. I'm a grown ass man who has failed and got back up to try again. I have been promoted, hired, fired, and disciplined. I have been sold out by coworkers. I have taken the blame for my team, even though I didn't have to. I have made mistakes, owned them, and paid the price. I have loyal employees to this day who would come work for me, and I have made my fair share of enemies along the way.

What did I learn? A lot. Above all, however, I learned to respect the chain of command, respectfully convey my message, and consider my audience. This book will offer lot of examples and stories where that may or may not have happened—and that is why it's in here.

This book is intended to help raise your self-awareness—to give you insights and thoughts on how to deal with the business world and the changes that occur daily in it. Most of all, it is to share what I know and help others not to make the mistakes I made along the way. I hope you find something valuable in all of this. Thank you.

Table of Contents

CHAPTER 1

What Does a Grown Ass Leader Look Like?

Guess what? There is no true example of what a grown ass leader looks like. However, there are certain qualities that all grown ass leaders/managers/owners will display to their employees, peers, and customers. These are everyday behaviors—not occasional behaviors when it's time for health and safety training. Honestly, it doesn't matter if you do or don't have these qualities, as they are merely daily examples of learned behavior and engrained into daily interaction; they are all something that, if you're not doing them now, you certainly can learn to do them easily if you CHOOSE to. Thus, I have listed a few examples of what a grown ass leader/manager/owner looks like

1. Makes Decisions: As a leader of others, no matter what title or spot in the chain you hold, you must make decisions daily, weekly, monthly, yearly. Believe it or not, your

decision-making is as simple as an employee asking if he or she can leave early on Thursday. How you handle that decision process speaks loudly and boldly to those you lead as well as to your peers and or supervisors. Do you just say "Yes, that's fine" and walk away? What did that decision tell others? That you don't care? That you don't care about your staff? That you don't care about Thursdays? Yes, it sounds stupid, but it is the result of the "Yeah, whatever" or "Yeah, that's fine" attitude. Deciding over something as simple as leaving early from a job can create giant ripples. Grown ass leaders/managers/owners will ask, "Why do you need to leave early on Thursday? Where are you in your assigned job duties that Thursday can handle you leaving early? Does this affect the efficiency of the team or department you oversee? Do you have others leaving early that day as well?" To most of us, asking these questions makes total sense. But truly look at yourself and ask how many times you have made a decision because it was easier. WAS IT THAT EASY? And if it was so easy, what type of effect came of that decision? Deciding isn't about giving out the answer; it's about determining the next best solution in order to not fail. We all want to be liked and respected by our staff; moreover, we all want to give our staff everything we possibly can.

How many of you trust but verify? How many of you say to yourself: "Not him. He/she has worked here for over 20 years"? Well, that decision just empowered that person to begin a pattern of poor work performance and output—and you are being manipulated by making quick and easy decisions. It's true that quick and easy decisions are made every day. But it's important that you widen your landscape of observation to see how such a decision will affect other staff, departments, and, most importantly, the needed results to stay employed.

Remember: You make the decision. You own the result and impact of that decision.

Story Time: I was an operations manager of 65 employees. The company I was working for was a seasonal company that ramped-up staff and ramped-down staff two times a year. Holidays are always sticky because everyone wants them off, as you know. So, knowing that the company is a spring and summer ramp-up, and Fourth of July is in the summer, what is the impact of the decision to let an employee off on the Fourth of July? I can tell you that one, and only one, out of the 65 got the Fourth of July off—and the ripple effect of that decision absolutely destroyed morale and team mentality. I had employees of less than a year as well as 35 years question the validity of that decision and why that person was chosen for the day off and not anyone else—especially after it was stated that nobody gets the day off. Now what you may not know is that my boss had allowed this same person to take the Fourth of July off every year, so it became expected. Well, how can you go against the instruction of your boss? Easy decision to make: employees get the Fourth of July off every year. Difficult to deal with the blast radius and its effect on the rest of your employees.

So, how can you deal with this in a decision-making process without going against the chain of command? Simple. Maybe have them work a longer day on the third to make the fourth a shorter day, wherein everyone leaves at noon. Come up with several possible solutions, like this one, to present to your superiors. In doing so, you take the thinking out of their hands: You have the buy-in of the staff; you maintain productivity; and you can take time to find a better solution. Not the easy quick solution, mind you. But, in the end, you did make a decision. You made a better one overall in the long run. If it works, the way you want, and the results are amazing, you will always own the decision. Leadership is about standing up and saying, "Okay. What is the next best solution?" How can WE make that happen?" Then, decision time: "Let's do it!"

2. Takes Action: Do what you say you are going to do! In his book *Meditations*, author Marcus Aurelius writes that action is the only truth. This book was written around 160 AD, and almost everything in the book is applicable today. How many companies, bosses, or employees have said one thing and done the opposite? I can tell you that I'm the hardest working person on Earth; yet, if I never SHOW it, then my action is the truth. My action of laziness is the truth. We all say things to make us sound amazing or better than others. But have you done what you can to SHOW your worth? In a world of servant leadership, which I'm a believer in, this will absolutely make you a better owner/leader/manager. Do what you say you're going to do! If you are a grown ass leader, then you will do what you say you will do.

   Story Time: I was consulting with a company. As I interviewed the location managers, each one of them stated: "We are all told that if we need anything to call the corporate office. When we call the corporate office, no one ever answers; when we leave a message, we never get a call back." Well, after several years of this, why would any of these location managers trust or believe anything the corporate office tells them? Even better, when I attended their convention, the corporate staff would give out their phone number and staff numbers to contact if you needed anything—and every one of the location managers just laughed and said "Why? You won't call us back."

ACTION IS THE ONLY TRUTH. We can say, "I'm available to you whenever you need me." But how many times have you not been available because you're busy or you just don't want to talk to that person? If someone thinks it's important enough to approach you with something, then it's important enough for you to pay attention. I'm a walk-n-talk person, but what does that action tell those who need my assistance? It should tell them that I'm constantly on the move and that they need to move with me in order to keep my attention. I can't say if that is the best way or not; it really depends on the situation and person. Your actions define you as a person, a leader, an owner, a manager. Your actions will let us know if you're a good person, bad person, person with an agenda, or you even one who knows what they're doing. Fake it until you make it doesn't work with action. Your actions will show if you are faking it.

Action must be genuine. Action must be who you are. It's so much easier to be yourself than pretending to be something or someone you're not. Ask any one of my clients from consulting and/or subordinates from my days as a leader and manager. They will tell you I preach that action is the only truth. I don't want you to tell me how great you are: Show me how great you are through your actions and the actions of the people you lead.

Story Time: I interviewed recently with a company for a position that was I was certainly qualified for and had a great interview. Here is where it gets bad. The interviewer was the head of the HR department, and the last 15 minutes of the interview was nothing but "Man, I have to get you in front of the owner. He will love you. I'm totally impressed..." and on and on. I left with "I will call you later today" and set up a time to come back and meet the owner. It's been over two months now, and he hasn't called back. Do what you say you are going to do. Why are we so afraid to communicate and do what we tell someone we are going to do? Why was he so afraid to call me and say it's not a good fit or some other BS that HR professionals love to give us when they have selected another candidate? It's not that difficult, and it's a sign of a poor leader when you can't do what you say you're going to do. In other words, you're a chicken; worse, if you are an HR leader, you have set a bad precedence for you and your company.

Which leads us to the next part of action is the only truth. The actions of those in your charge also reflect directly on you. If you take appropriate action, then they will also because you are setting the standard. If your action is lazy and you make quick decisions, so will they. Your actions are not only yours to be genuine, they are yours to show your staff, department, or whomever the standard with which performance is expected. You must ensure that your actions set a proper example for your team to follow. There is no longer a place for "Do as I say not as I do." The people you manage or lead want and need your actions to lead, guide, inspire, teach, train, and develop them. Do not fail them—for if they fail, so do you as their leader.

3. Holds Self Twice as Accountable as Any Other: A grown ass leader has one great fear, a fear that will drive them to do the right things in the right situations. This fear is a fear of failure. Grown ass people only want what is best for them and the people they lead and serve. This applies to life as well as business. In order to control that fear, great leaders hold themselves twice as accountable as they hold their staff,

department, or team. Accountability must be 360 degrees. A leader will not only hold you accountable but hold him or herself accountable as well.

Story Time: When I was with a company, we had a corporate meeting in January to discuss the previous year's performance and coming year's expectations. As the leader of the company's entire operational unit, I stood up with four of my management staff and laid out our plan and expected results. I stood in front of a board of directors with expectations of growth and profitability. In December of that same year, I flew to company headquarters and stood in front of that same board of directors—only this time with results and performance that were below what I stated that I, and my location, would deliver. In fact, it was terrible. I stood up with my senior staff and said here is what we did and why I made certain decisions.

"If anyone needs to be fired it's me," I said.

"This team killed itself everyday along with me to ensure that we met our projected profit performance. I made the decisions, and they did what I asked them to. They should not be held accountable for what I instructed them to do. I am ultimately responsible, and I stand here to tell you if you need to fire anyone it should be me. They should not be disciplined in anyway but learn from this year and succeed next year."

As I left the room and took the elevator to the main entrance to leave for the airport, I wholly expected to be let go and have to pay my way home. Well, the CEO came out while I was waiting for my Uber and said to me, "I wish I had 50 of you in our corporate office. Go back home with your team and make next year the best ever." Not only did I hold myself twice as accountable as my team, but, after I made it home, my team was more than inspired to not let poor performance happen again knowing that this is a WE effort not a THEM effort. They knew I would stand in front of them and take all of the blame and none of the praise.

That is holding yourself accountable. Are you willing to lose your job for the performance of your team? If you don't hold yourself twice as accountable as you hold your team, then are you willing to lose your job over them? Accountability is simple. Here is the expected result; here is the expected action to achieve that result; here is the timeline to do it in:

<u>EVERY DECISION FROM HERE ON OUT MUST POSITIVELY IMPACT THE RESULTS NEEDED.</u>

As a grown ass leader/owner/manager, you must make sure that this decree is followed. You developed a profit plan or maybe you didn't, but your actions and the actions of your team must be measured and accounted for in order to achieve your profit or performance goals. Failure to maintain this accountability is the kiss of death.

4. Listens & Observes: Many a leader has always looked at him or herself as the keeper of all the knowledge and the answers. Then, when the time presents itself, that leader downloads this information to those they deem need it. While some of these previous statements are true as a leader/owner/manager, you must share your knowledge and experience to ensure the success of others, which in turn becomes your success. But what about when it goes sideways, and you need to implement behavior change or operational SOP change? What do you do then? Do you continue to download information in the hopes that they all understand and will execute

your decision as you exactly need? Give poor direction, get poor result. A leader's greatest assets are many, but two that are often forgotten are the power of observation and the power of listening. I learned growing up, as we all probably did, to trust our gut. Where does our gut get its information? From what we see and what we hear. So why do we often not trust the input that our own senses give us?

Observation is one part. Use your eyes to gather input. In the movie *The Replacements*, before the final game, Keanu Reeves is sitting in an empty football stadium. The coach, played by Gene Hackman, asks him what he is doing. Keanu replies, "I'm watching the game." This statement is not only powerful in the sense of planning and preparing for the ebbs and flows of success and failure and what actions you will take to adjust to the changing tides. It also sends a powerful message regarding observation. He's not only watching the game, but he's watching what his team is doing and where it is succeeding and failing and where he can help. He is also observing the other team: What it is doing; how it will adjust to its adaptations. The power of observation is too often forgotten. As a consultant, I would tell owners that there will be days that you just need to step away and watch your staff work. Do not interfere because it is working, the way it should. Your interference will just slow it down.

Observation is also important with assigning tasks—or corrective conversation is needed. Your ability to observe nonverbal communication, behavior, and, more importantly, reactions to your decisions or outcomes can be powerful. Does the reaction show a unified team, or do you have a single cancer growing that is going against the company's goal or agenda? When you assign tasks or delegate responsibility, what reaction do you get from the assigned person? Sometimes it's not what I asked you to do, but it's how you reacted when I asked. Do not be afraid to trust what you see. Remember, too, that action is the only truth. Use the power of observation to ensure that the action is the true person and true behavior. Every action must make a positive impact on the performance and profit goals. Do not be afraid to step away for a moment to observe what is going on in your operations or department. That information is extremely powerful for problem solving and for finding the next best solution. Trust yourself enough to be able to take the time to observe and use that observation to make the best decisions.

5. Listening. As an owner/leader/manager, listening is one of your greatest assets. Listening isn't just hearing what people tell you or say. Listening is allowing yourself to internalize constructive criticism, disagreements as improvements, and issues as opportunities. Listening will allow you to ask the right questions to lead yourself and your staff to the best possible solution. I was told once that, if your team isn't regularly and passionately disagreeing with you, you may not be creating a safe environment for the necessary conflict to produce the most refined strategies. This means that you must be strong enough to swallow that criticism knowing that it's not personal—it's for the betterment of performance.

Allowing yourself to listen to what they are really saying. Weed through the emotion and get to the facts. Listening will give you that opportunity.

Listening will allow you to ask the right questions. Just like making easy decisions, if you have the answer and just listen to a question and give and answer, is it done? What about walking the staff down the road to a solution by listening to what they are really asking and ask a follow-up question to create thinking. Ask questions to ensure the staff is listening. Ask questions to see if the staff thinks the same way you are or the same way as the company. The right question and the right listening will give you an ample amount of information for you to make the best possible decision and or solution.

eyes and ears are the two best tools a leader has

6. Encourages & Embraces Feedback: Feedback comes in all ways in every direction. Grown ass leaders encourage this feedback and view it as an opportunity to improve. Also, feedback as stated above should be encouraged. You should be available and prepared to listen, observe, hold yourself accountable, make decisions, and take appropriate action. This will invite feedback.

Story Time: As a manager of multiple locations, I once realized that I was disconnected from the store life and stuck in the corporate life mentality. Fact is, especially in retail environments, you hear this a lot. "They have been out of the stores too long; they don't know what it's like day to day in the stores." That does happen, and I have stated that membership has its privileges. However, I had a meeting with 13 of my managers, and all I did was let them tell me what they need from me, what I'm doing right, and what I'm doing wrong. The first time was terrible; they were all afraid to speak. Once it got going, though, the feedback was honest and passionate. I sat and listened and promised not to argue or disagree. Again, if it is important enough for them to bring it to my attention, then it's important enough for me to take it seriously. At the end of the third meeting, where I allowed my staff to give me open feedback in any form or fashion, I began to realize what management techniques worked for my staff and what didn't. What I thought I was doing that worked wasn't working and, most importantly, how to motivate, improve, teach, train, and develop them as future managers and leaders. You must be a tough-skinned grown ass leader in order to take any and all feedback and make it an opportunity to improve performance and profit.

In closing this chapter, I want you to be able to look at yourself in the mirror and truly tell yourself, "I am a grown ass leader who is willing to stand with my team when I need to, to take a bullet for them. To teach train and develop them. To make the tough decisions that should make the team and the performance outcome better." These are not the end-all. In fact, I could write an entire book on leadership qualities. This is just a few of the top-level examples. The other qualities and skills will be present if these five are already there.

You and I don't possess these skills all of the time. We get caught up in the day-to-day grind. But, hopefully, this will help make you more self-aware of the times that you are not being a grown ass leader.

So, what should I take away from this chapter? First, I hate the term "take away." It immediately makes me think of homework. I hated homework when I was a kid, and I hate it now that I'm an adult. So, at the end of each chapter, I will ask you to find your call to action. This way, we can put some of the thoughts and ideas that are bouncing around after reading this to use. Action is the only truth, so why not take action? So, for this chapter on, what does a grown ass adult look like? My call to action for you is to find just one of the qualities or skills that I wrote about and relate them to you and your skill set or your behaviors. If you can make that connection, then you are gaining—and the more you connect, the more you gain, and now you're gaining momentum. Keep that momentum and refer back to anything you need to keep moving forward. Remember there are many qualities and behaviors; you may only possess one or none; in that case, however, now you have a starting point—and we all have to start somewhere. Why not start here? Why not start now?

CHAPTER 2

Idiots Versus Morons

As a business consultant, newly hired leader, or newly promoted manager, I found one thing always present in a new position or title: there are always more experienced people in a department, staff, or company; these are the more experienced and tenured people who have survived the evolution of the company and have become a wealth of knowledge. You are not the new young gun, so to speak, and what do you know about this business? A grown ass leader does not know everything and doesn't claim to know everything—but he or she is always willing to learn and get better.

My clients who are reading this will laugh because I have done this exercise numerous times with them. It allows a new or newer less-experienced person to establish him or herself as someone who knows how to be successful—and not the smartest person in the room.

As an owner/leader/manager of those who have an established and experienced staff, the kiss of death is to say: "This is the way we have always done this." I love hearing this statement because it tells me that the business and the performance have not adapted to the changing tides of the business world and the changes it brings daily. So, as we begin the exercise of idiots versus morons, please remember one thing: Do not take the negative connation of terms personally. It is merely to show two separate ways of thinking and leading a company, department, or staff.

So, let's begin. There are two types of people in the world. Who are they? Men and women, rich and poor, college educated and not college educated? No. None of those. The answer is idiots and morons.

What is the difference between the two?

Idiots: First, let me say that we are all idiots multiple times in our lives. We are all well-informed and subject-matter experts at something. But that doesn't mean we know everything. In fact, it means we know what we know, but we don't know what we don't know. Many times, we revert back to what we know in order to survive. That is idiotic because, when we do that, we stop learning, listening, and adapting to the changes in our environment.

Common ways to spot an idiot are to hear: "I got this. Yeah, I know. Okay, I'm on it. Yes, I know how to do my job." These common responses should blip your radar, and you need to start asking questions and following up on the expectations and results. Idiots are the smartest persons in the room; they know everything about everything; they want to get the job done so that you can praise them for a job well done and on time. Idiots will tell you you're wrong in a myriad of ways. Whether it's to offer a better solution or just flat-out tell you you're wrong.

Story Time: I was consulting with a company that had -8% performance for the year so far and wanted to course-correct before the halfway mark of the year. As I sat in a conference room listening to a new vice president of operations discuss the plan on how to start making positive impacts on this performance, she was interrupted and told, "No that's not going to work; that isn't our job." Several times it was openly stated in a group setting, "No, you're wrong." Now, not only is this extremely disrespectful, but my question to the three operations managers, who were obviously the smartest people in the room: "If none of this works, then what are your solutions. And, if you have a solution, why haven't you tried it already and be a leader who brings positive results?" If you're not offering solutions, then all you are doing is complaining.

Most idiots have stopped learning, stopped listening, stopped adapting. How many businesses are successful for 10 years then lose money for three? The reason they do is because they have become idiots. Either because of changes in the operational landscape of technology, they just get in a groove and their staff gets complacent. There are numerous reasons, but the common denominator is that the leadership team has become a bunch of idiots. We know what we are doing—it has worked for 10 years, so why change? When your performance suffers, what are you going to do? They will most likely work IN their business instead of work ON their business. So, rather than learn, ask questions, and adapt, they work longer hours, do the work that they pay other people to do, or, in some cases, go out and do the actual day-to-day field work.

Stop being an idiot.

Idiots also have extreme amount of pride. Every decision they make is the greatest decision ever. The decision will impact the business immediately and will solve all the world's problems. Idiots do not like to fail and hate being wrong. Refer to my previous story with the operations managers. After I questioned what solutions they had and what they had done to correct performance, I was immediately the enemy, and they aligned themselves to try to beat me or get me fired as the consultant. Guess what? Idiots are also easy to spot and easy to defeat. If you want to correct an idiot and get him/her to back up and start thinking differently, just keep asking questions. If you don't know what question to ask, just ask the idiot WHY? Idiots will not have any good answers to any questions. They will be, "That's the way we always do things" or "That's the way I was trained." Funny how we started the idiots versus moron's conversation with "That's the way we have always done it."

Remember: We are all idiots—and, again, I am trying to help you to be more self-aware of that idiotic behavior and step back and say, "Maybe I should listen; maybe I should ask a question; maybe I'm not right." Most importantly, I'm not the smartest guy in the room. By the way, at last update, the company that I was consulting for will end the year with a 20% decrease in business from the previous year; it fired the CEO and CFO, and the VP left after only six months. Maybe it has more idiots in its leadership team than we think.

So here is an important question that you must ask if you haven't already. How do I get an idiot to realize he/she is an idiot and has become more of a moron? Remember, idiots have all the answers and are never wrong. They know everything. So how do you get them to realize they are idiots? You can't come out and tell them. That will shut them down and create an enemy. So, use this exercise. Take a large 3M easel pad and make a T-square with it

Task	Time	$	*

Have the person list every activity he/she does every day for an entire week, minus breaks, bathroom, smoke, etc. We only want job-related activities. Remember, only let them tell you what they do. List all activities first; then, go to how much time each week it takes to do the tasks. Then, ask does the task make sales/profit for the company or does it improve output or efficiency. If it does, don't be afraid to use multiple symbols to show the importance. Total the time and see what they say are the total hours they work in a week. Look at the value of the activities in either dollars or efficiency. Then, ask this one simple question: Are you doing everything to reach your goals?

It's both a thought question and a question to challenge that person's answers. No more of this "I'm doing what I'm told to do; I am doing what the company needs me to do." This little exercise will show that, usually, there are activities that they spend a lot of time on that don't do anything for profitability or efficiency. They do tasks that they can certainly delegate to others. They do activities that total 60–70 hours of work a week, and they only want to work 40. Or, and this has happened, they outright lie to you and make it look like they are irreplaceable and do everything. If that is the case, then go back to the basic questions. Why? Remember to ask questions and, if you don't know what to ask, just keep asking why. The truth will emerge.

Now, once you do this activity, and the idiot realizes, using his/her own words and answers, that he/she is actually not right, this idiot will no longer want to be around you. Most idiots hate being wrong, so they will excuse themselves or get mad or have some type of reaction that you will be able to see either verbally or nonverbally. Let them have their time to think inward; hopefully, this "punch in the stomach" will allow them to start understanding what you are trying to do to them—not beat them up but to get them to think bigger, act bigger, and own their decisions.

Now we have to address the other side of this behavior: morons. Keep in mind to take away the negative connotation of the word "moron," as I will explain the reason why it's actually a smart move to be a moron.

Morons: Okay, so let's talk about morons. Let me start you thinking about why you want to be a moron with this exercise. There are 10 people in the room, all experts in their field. You ask them to put together a bike, which none of them have had the education or training to do. Who is the smartest person in the room? It's the person who raises his/her hand and says, "I need help. I don't know what to do." This person may be a rocket scientist or an electrical engineer, but he/she doesn't know how to put a bike together. But this person is the smartest person in the room because he/she asked for help. This person asked for knowledge.

If you own a business, let me just say a great number of morons will make your operation perform so much better than a great number of idiots. Morons will always learn and want to learn. They will learn and then improve and see if they can relearn. The more information, training, and data you provide for them, the more they want and the more they will perform. Morons are constantly asking how can we improve. Why can't we try this or that? Morons can be an employee who has worked for a company for 40 years but still comes to work and says teach me what I don't know, help me learn what I need to. Remember that, 25 years ago, technology didn't exist that does today, and those employees must be willing to learn the new equipment or process in order for the company to adapt and maintain.

Morons have a great quality that we all possess, but it gets tucked away as we go through life. They continue to ask questions and, most importantly, they ask WHY. Remember when you were a kid and you constantly barraged your parents with why questions, and they would give you answers. If they didn't answer, you kept asking until you got an answer; if you didn't like the answer, you kept asking again and again and again and again. As leaders/owners/managers of others, we need that skill. Think of it this way. When an employee is late, do you ask why he/she was late? Do you follow up with questions to make sure you are getting all of the facts? Remember, I said earlier to ask questions and continue to ask questions. If you don't know what to ask, then ask why.

Leader/owners/managers want morons on their team. They want people who will ask the right questions in order to drill down to the root cause and will assist in the creation of the best solution. Morons will work with you and not against you. Morons will never openly disagree with you and/or disrespect the chain of command. Morons are very aware of their job purview but also, more often than not, have no issues working as a team to get the best result. Morons are so much more coachable, teachable, trainable. They thirst for knowledge and leadership. A great team of morons will make you look great as a manager or leader. They will offer solutions and keep you on your toes to ensure that you are developing them. Guess what? The more they learn and grow, the greater the chance you will get promoted because you have a stable of staff who can take your place.

So, there you go, however you do the exercise. I've done it differently every time. You have to mold it to your audience and its skill level and level of importance in the chain. I have done this exercise within all levels of a company—from the secretary to the owner to the board of directors. I promised each one of them that, by the end, they will all want to be morons. They all start asking questions of themselves, of their management team, of their staff. They all become more self-aware of their words and actions and the impact they have on the performance and profit of the business. They all realize that they must stop giving orders and teach, train, and develop.

Remember, we will all be idiots at some point over some topic that we are educated and experts in. If you train yourself to constantly ask questions, your leadership will be stronger because your solutions will be presented in a manner of the team finding the solution—not that you didn't tell us the solution.

<u>Call to action for this chapter</u>. Simple, you are going to be an idiot and a moron. You will move back and forth between these two like a pendulum. Do your best to be self-aware of when you are being an idiot. Don't be afraid to be called out as an idiot. It's damn near impossible to pick a side and stay on that side. We all have the thing that we are really good at or really smart at, so that leads us to being an idiot. Also, failure is an option in this regard. You can fail at being an idiot, and you can fail at being a moron. The beauty of this exercise is that either side can be victorious, as long as you don't end up on the end of the spectrum. The closer to the middle you stay, the

closer you are to being an idiot and a moron and gain the best of both sides. My call to action for you is to find your center of both an idiot and a moron. Stay away from the ends of the spectrum. Also never be afraid to use this exercise to establish your credibility.

CHAPTER 3

VDM and Land Mines

The term "Vantasner Danger Meridian" (VDM) is derived from the Amazon Prime Series *Patriot* (I highly recommend the series). What strikes me about the series is the ideals of the VDM, i.e., land mines are everywhere, and you will step on one or two or more in your lifetime. Further, if you are over halfway through an operation, it actually takes a longer time and more energy to turn around and go back to where you started than it is to move forward.

In its simplest form, Vantasner Danger Meridian is this. How can you survive a land mine without turning back but continuing to move forward and minimizing the damage by moving forward and completing the operation? As noted, you will step on land mines throughout your career as an owner/leader/manager. Sometimes you will do it intentionally; sometimes it happens due to your location and or the landscape you operate in. Finally, you will step on land mines due to the people that you are leading. Not all of them are on your side and want to see you succeed. They will place you in front of as many land mines as possible and will try to guide and direct you into stepping on them.

Bang! You just stepped on a land mine. Now what? I can tell you firsthand I have stepped on land mines, intentionally and accidentally. I have stepped on land mines and survived—and I've been blown up.

There is no better teacher than experience and mistakes. Consider me experienced. So back to your land mine. It's scary. It endangers your livelihood, career, and ability to earn money. So how to you use the VDM to get through the explosion with the minimal amount of damage and harm to yourself or to your team? Question number one is what is the exit strategy if there is one? If not, we need one immediately. The exit strategy is *not* to get away from the situation and isolate yourself but to finish the operation and come out the other side unharmed or minimally damaged. Always remember that truth and transparency must be a part of a strategy as well as facts—not emotions.

Story Time: I was an operations manager for a company, in charge of several departments, all of whom depended on each other to maximize performance and profitability. So, at the beginning of the busy season, I made a decision to focus on one department rather than the other two due to the fact that this department was priority as far as performance and had the greatest impact on overall performance. Halfway through the busy season, the land mine exploded. I have to answer to ownership of why was this department staffed and why these two departments were suffering. I made the decision to focus my energy on the department I felt was the constraint but neglected to remember that the constraint always moves throughout the organization. I had to sit in front of the VP for the region, the CEO, and my manager and say, "I MADE THE DECISION TO DO THIS." I made the decision to focus here. I also instructed my team to do the following things to ensure that the other departments were still moving forward, even though I wasn't in their department daily. At the end of that busy season, I called my managers into a conference room and told them all that they survived the season and did a great job. I also told them I would be terminated due to the poor performance. Whether self-fulfilling prophecy or not, I was let go. I minimized the damage by not allowing the land mine blast to affect the team, even though I took a direct hit.

Land mines like this are easy to spot and easy to step on. Customer complaints, language you use, and the big one of sexual harassment are the easiest to see, yet they continue to get stepped on daily. Realize that, in any decision or operation, you will start down a path that, once you're past halfway and it's not working the way it should, you have stepped on the land mine and the damage is done. It's longer and harder to go back the way you came, and many times it doesn't do any good, so you must move forward and minimize the damage of the land mine. That is the Vantasner Danger Meridian. You can create a leadership style by using this philosophy. You can train your team to use this philosophy as well.

VDM leadership allows for acknowledgment of land mines and to pre-plan and strategize to move through and around them before heading down the road or operation. Major questions to ask yourself and your staff: As we begin this mission, do we have clear guidelines for our actions? Does the entire team? Widen the landscape to find the VDM that will allow to move forward?

We all know the 5 Ps: prior proper planning prevents poor performance. The VDM is exactly the same. You constantly are thinking what if, then what, and repeat what if, then what. When I was a district manager, as I would travel in between stores, I would always app the time in traffic (in Atlanta) by talking to myself about what if Gary quits? Who do I have to take his place? If I move Linda to Gary's spot, then who do I have to replace Linda? Am I promoting? Am I recruiting? I would go through as many scenarios as possible so that, if and when anything changes, I was prepared. As a leader when a land mine explodes or the road takes a sudden turn, you run around with your hair on fire; you lose confidence and credibility from your team. You must maintain a calm and decisive demeanor. How can you do that if you don't know what you're going to do when things change or a land mine explodes? This quality and prior planning are easy to teach, train, and develop when you are in a company with a multilevel structure. You teach, train, and develop by letting your managers think the same way. I did this by going to my strong managers and saying who are the best employees and what are they going to do if they leave or if I take them out of your store and put them in another store. How will I replace them without losing momentum or productivity? I had store managers and assistant store managers. What if I promote your assistant? Who is ready to be promoted in your store or outside of your store? In retail, it is easy to apply the VDM. I worked retail for many years, and my number one strategy was always, "Well, if so and so doesn't come to work, then who covers their spot and who moves to backfill, so we can get done what needs to get done?" That is VDM in its simplest and smartest form.

Vantasner Danger Meridian.

So, we have properly planned prior to the land mine exploding, but a land mine we didn't expect just exploded. So now what? First, acknowledge the land mines and/or identify them, how they exploded, and who stepped on them. At some point, as a leader or manager, you cannot accept repeat negative impacting behavior. The first thing to do, then, is to widen the landscape that we can draw information from. By this, I mean examine sales issues by looking at operation or HR solutions. Don't pigeonhole your thinking. Solutions exist everywhere; yet, we miss them sometimes because they don't fit perfectly into the box. We need them to.

Story Time: As a plant manager, I had an overage of drivers and a shortage of dock workers. In order to keep productivity going until I could get more dock workers, every new driver I hired had to work a week on the dock, so they could learn and understand the dock. This helped get me temporary help on the dock as well as keep drivers working when there weren't enough trucks to drive or routes to be run. A secondary benefit is that I get cross-training; a tertiary benefit is that now the drivers understand the dock workers' job, how hard it actually is, and will appreciate each other's work and their part of the overall process and impact. Thus, in this case, I used a wide landscape to find the next best solution.

Next in the search for the next best solution, we need to find what will allow us to keep moving forward and minimizing the damage. We also need to widen the landscape to ensure the actual blast radius of the land mine is covered. Many times, a land mine doesn't just affect you, your team, or your department. It crosses over into other departments. How many times have you had a high-level incident and changes come down the pipe, and you sit back and think how does this help us? It actually creates more work for us. Widen your landscape. Make sure the perfect action doesn't create six other problems in four other departments. Then, it's not the best solution. Thus, include who you need to, no matter what department to find the next best solution. Also use your professional network. With all the social media apps and connections, we no longer need to be afraid to post or reach out to a subject matter expert, i.e., reach out to anyone and everyone you need to in order to find the next best solution. The goal here is, again, the VDM. How do we minimize the damage after the blast has happened? This includes other companies. Again, with social media and online apps, we can build a base and build a strategy based on other people's land mines and how they maneuvered the VDM and came out of it. When you are applying the VDM, nothing is off-limits to research or investigate for the next best solution.

Finally, the VDM does have a point in that you need to execute the solution of execution. Termination of an employee is the next best solution if this individual continues to step on land mines and not improve based on education, teaching, training, and development. At some point, accountability has to come into play, and the VDM is to remove the problem. As a consultant, I used to coach owners on the two ways to get rid of cancer: cut it out and terminate or chemotherapy, which is tolerating and documenting until you've had enough. If the individual who keeps putting the VDM into play isn't properly documented by the time you decide to cut out the cancer, then you can't use it. You will have to put up with it through chemo because you haven't properly documented behaviors and results. As discussed in previous chapters, accountability comes into play every day with every action. You must consider the VDM for these actions and the actions of your team.

Story Time: I was a district manager and had a manager who was not completing the correct paperwork to hire employees and keep in compliance. During the counseling session, he decided to blame-shift rather than hold himself accountable. Not only did he step on an HR documentation land mine, he decided to step on another by challenging the director of HR during his counseling session and blamed her for the mess. Two land mines in less than two hours. So, as we did the documentation, it was expressly written that further violations of this policy will result in discipline up to and including termination. Not more than 60 days later, I pulled up to his store with his replacement. When I approached the store, he met me outside and asked "So I'm terminated?" Yes, and we talked about if it happened again you would be. Too many instances of the same mistake.

There are only so many land mines that can be stepped on before you, as the boss, will be in the middle of a VDM and that VDM will end in termination or personnel change. Remember, too, your inaction of a VDM may cause your boss to initiate his/her VDM, which may cost you your ability to earn a wage. Remember to also do your best to have a VDM ready for most of your visible land mines in your operation's landscape. Also remember to own your actions and the actions of those you are a leader of. Vantasner Danger Meridian is a real tool. It can be trained, taught, and developed in everyone at any time. Planning your VDM in all forms and fashions will eliminate stresses in your career and will put you in a position of poise in a time of panic. It will elevate you above the noise and gossip and show your true leadership ability.

For this chapter, the call to action will be to do your best to identify and avoid land mines—at least the ones you can avoid. Respect the process and always work on your VDM as much as possible. Be open and honest if the explosion happens and keep everyone in the know. The best thing you can do is to not run around with your hair on fire when things explode. If you panic, you have failed in the creation and implementation of your VDM. Guess what? Your team or the people you lead will also panic. When we panic, we make emotional decisions not rational ones. That is the importance of the VDM. Stay in the moment and stay on course.

CHAPTER 4

Accountability

This is not a repeat of the quality possessed by a grown ass leader, grown ass manager, or grown ass person. This will help you be accountable as a leader and a grown ass leader when those around you act like children. I will remind you that accountability is not only being accountable to your actions but the actions of everyone that you lead, manage, and supervise. The hardest part of this is the fact that your subordinates will act like children in order to get what they want or push their agenda. You will get caught up in that, and it will destroy your accountability. It gives them the power and takes away every tool you have in your tool box to be a successful leader. Why not just shut down all that noise with accountability questions?

How does one continue to maintain accountability when everyone else are acting like children? Accountability! Accountability of actions, performance, expectations, company culture. Do not ever be afraid to put a number on any or all of these. You can do it without being a tyrant or A-hole to your staff. Yes, you will need to be firm and fair. You will need to assess the situation, though you cannot waver from the accountable measurable that is set by you or your company leadership. So, let's get into it.

Rule 1: It starts in the beginning—from the day you hire someone or someone is assigned to your department. You have to set time aside to sit down with this individual and set your MEASURABLE performance metrics: set the measurable attendance metrics; set the measurable professional metrics. Not doing this is not only a disservice to that employee, but it sets him/her up for failure and sets you on a course of failed expectations and performance. Leave no detail out. Be sure to cover everything that is a part of the daily performance expectation. You must have a measurable to hold accountable to, i.e., if you need to make 100 sales calls a day, then the expectation is 100 calls. If the day starts at 8 a.m., then the expectation is that you are in the building, on the clock, and working at 8 a.m. If you are assigned a deadline, meet it. If you send an email asking for a response, give a timeframe. Remember not responding is a response. Put these expectations in writing as well. Documentation will save your life. We all see job descriptions, but we need to make sure we document and communicate job expectations. How easy is it now to ask your staff: "Did you make your 100 sales calls?" instead of asking, "Did you have a good day? Did you do a good job?" We have to meet and exceed expectations and performance. This allows one to deal in facts not emotions.

Rule 2: Checkpoint Charlie. You will have annual expectations. But if you wait until month 11 of 12 months to hold people accountable, then guess what? You are an idiot and you will not succeed. That land mine will take your job status and the respect of everyone you lead. Checkpoint Charlie needs to be established to stay in front of performance—not wait for it to fail, then course correct, based on the priority and importance of the measurable and its impact on the profitability. The greater the priority and its impact on profitability, the greater the frequency of Checkpoint Charlie. Weekly, monthly, quarterly, and even daily if necessary. By the way, if you say you're going to check on metrics in a certain time frame—THEN DO IT! Nothing will create poor performance than not following through on what you say you are going to do. Also remember that, when you have a Checkpoint Charlie, you will need a plan of action to either correct or promote the actions and behaviors. If you need to course correct, then what correction is needed? Is it a correction of process or behavior? Is the correction needed because a land mine got stepped on? Remember that Checkpoint Charlie is needed because it prevents a situation from sneaking up on us. It prevents digging a hole so deep that you can't get back to level. Checkpoint Charlie is a valuable asset to accountability for you and your staff. After about three checkpoint Charlies, your staff will have the information you need ready for you as well as being prepared to discuss the action plan if they missed on their expected results or metrics. When this happens, you had a team that is working in combination with each other, knowing that the team will be asked about your day and the answer isn't "just good."

Rule 3: Observe and Listen. As a grown ass leader/manager/professional, you have to use the greatest tools at your disposal: your eyes and your ears. Using the first two rules, you know what the expectation is, you know when the Checkpoint Charlie will be, so now you need to listen and observe the actions and behaviors. This will help you to develop a correction based on the input you have and match that to the correction that your staff will offer. If you have an employee who shows up five minutes late every day and always say that he/she is too busy to finish anything completely, what did you observe and hear that you can use for your Checkpoint Charlie correction to get that employee to the desired performance? The easiest one is smokers. How many smoke breaks do they take in a day and yet they are overwhelmed with too much work and too little time? On average, one hour of work time is lost due to multiple smoke breaks. Your observation of how many and how long is essential to correcting the behavior. It allows you to challenge the excuses with facts. The power of observation and listening will give you enormous amounts of data. This data will only strengthen your position in a disagreement on why an objective wasn't met. If you are doing the activity required, then why was the metric not met? You can't go into that discussion if you have nothing to refer to that proves your point.

Story Time: When I was a regional manager, I would go to stores to visit with the district manager or other field staff. As we entered a location, the field staff would gravitate to its area expertise and begin downloading its knowledge to correct or assist or complement the performance they observed. I would stand in the back of the location and just observe and listen to the employees and management. I would take notes of things I saw and heard. I got more information out of just standing in the back and using my tools. I knew what the manager needed help with. I certainly got a great handle on customer service in the store as well as structure in the store and how well the store manager was managing the people and the tasks they were assigned. I can hear the gossip. I can identify which employees are bought in and which aren't. I can observe communication skills and styles to see if they work or not. I can see organization as well as what problems are in the store right now and if the management team has its arms around those problems—or do I and other field staff need to step in to get the team back to zero and stay level? I even used to sit in my car and observe how many smokers would take breaks outside and for how long. Using all of this, I can create action plans that will improve operation and correct negative impact behaviors. It's so easy, and we all do it; we just don't focus on the input it gives us.

Rule 4: Execute. Do what you say you're going to do. Accountability is so easily turned against you if you don't do what you say you're going to do. If you have set expectations and the consequences for not meeting expectations, then execute them. You're not being a jerk, or a mean boss, or a tyrant. You're holding everyone, including yourself, accountable. I fully understand the hardest thing to hold people accountable for is attendance, yet it's the easiest to measure. Why is it so hard? Well, if we widen our landscape, we see that the employee pool to hire from is not what employers are wanting and you justify poor behavior like attendance issues because at least they show up, and they are still better than anyone you could hire today. You have just thrown accountability out the window. You will see poor performance become the norm, and profit will disappear in time. I can't say when or how long, but it will happen. Employees will see that there is no consequence for being late; they know that you will tolerate it because you can't hire just anyone to do the job. Then what? The next step is taking money or taking product or abusing all policies that you have, knowing that if you let one get away you will let them all. Remember great leaders are liked; they are respected. Remember that anything you measure will show an improvement. Inspect what you expect. Remember in Chapter One that we discussed holding yourself accountable. This is not a repeat of that; this chapter is about holding your team and others accountable—without lowering yourself to their level when they begin to act like children and throw tantrums. You must stay above the noise and emotion. That is why we say facts not emotions. The facts have been collected in multiple ways, of course, and we are ready for anything they come at us with. Most of all, never be afraid to hold your staff accountable. You fail them, and they will fail you if you don't. If you are feeling afraid, it is most likely because you don't have the correct facts to hold them accountable. You may not trust the facts, so double-check them to make sure. You certainly don't want to hold someone accountable and then have your data proven false. That is a mortal wound to your leadership and credibility.

Accountability is a difficult behavior to master. Call to action is to master this skill. Human nature in our DNA makes us want to blame-shift or deflect away from us, especially if we are in a stressful or disciplinary situation. You must remember that accountability is measured and starts with day one. You cannot be a nice guy when you hold people accountable. I've done that, and it fails miserably. You can be overbearing with your accountability as well and be a tyrant. Remember to manage the measurables and keep to your schedule. This is hard work, but it's easier than updating your résumé every few years.

CHAPTER 5

What's Right Is Right

One of my all-time favorite sayings is: what's right is right. The difficult part is that the huge majority of the time doing what is right and making the right decision is the most difficult thing to do. Why? There are many reasons why, and they all lead back to one point. AGENDAS! Agendas are a cancer that destroy everything they touch. Personal or professional, an agenda that is not in line with company goals or initiatives will result in failure. Personal agendas, bottom line, get people fired. Agendas are everywhere. They are destructive, period. They will hide in plain sight so not to be noticed. They will lie in wait, and when they finally show themselves it is way past too late. Agendas are driven from human experience and emotion; from my experience, however, I see most of them care focused on greed, envy, and pride. Three of the seven deadly sins are the most powerful agenda creators and drive the individual to execute his/her agenda in any way that will work. This person will chase the title, the status, the power, the recognition, and, of course, the money. So, let's start with high-level agendas.

Company agendas are built to ensure there is clear direction and expectations for all members of the company and their goals. Consider this agenda a highway. It has on-ramps and off-ramps. The company agenda is heading in a certain direction. As you bring on new employees or promote an employee to a new position, your also bring along his/her personal attributes, behaviors, nuances, and agendas. These should all merge on the highway and work into the flow of the company. You don't have to be going the same speed, but you certainly need to be moving in the same direction. So, when this new injection merges on the highway and that agenda is going against the flow of traffic on that highway, what is going to happen? A wrong-way driver causes a major crash and loss of life—in this case, it's loss of profit or job. When you identify an agenda that goes against the company agenda, you must act immediately before that agenda destroys your hard work, your department's or staff's hard work, and costs the company profit.

Every department has an agenda and its highway. These should all merge to make the company agenda, which allows traffic to move at the most efficient performance. A wrong-way agenda in any department at any level can be destructive. So, what is the company agenda, and is it a negative agenda? Most company agendas are simple: Get work; do work. Get paid for the work you did. Take care of your people, and they will take care of the customers. More customers; more profit. Most employees just want to do the best job they can and be recognized. You rarely if ever hire a bad employee; they are created and developed over time and, through their experiences, typically begin to form their agenda—and that is when it becomes destructive. As a leader and using your leadership skills and tools, how can identify this agenda? First, let's remember to use our tools. Listen to your staff. If you have someone who continuously talks about how he/she is going to do things when in charge or how this person would have handled a situation, it should set off your alarm and raise your awareness. He/she is showing an agenda, and it may not be in line with the company or department agenda.

Story Time: I was working for a regional retail chain store. It was family-owned and ran, with locations in five states. The headquarters was in the same city as the store I worked in. There was a store manager who worked at a store that had legal trouble and lost its ability to sell beer due to selling to underage customers. This same manager also ran a store that I worked at when I was an assistant manager. This manager's name was Gary, and Gary had a personal agenda of wanting to be in charge of everyone. He chased any title that gave him power over people. He loved titles that gave him the chance to hire and fire and be the high-ranking executive that he felt he should be. This manager blame-shifted everything onto his people, saying anything that was wrong was their fault and any successes were his alone. After he lost the beer license for his store, he applied for a job in the company and headquarters in the HR department; on the same day he put his name in the hat, he accused three other store managers, his peers, of being racist and using race to treat him differently. He, of course, was hired into the HR department. Six months later, the HR department was all the same gender and race as him. He surrounded himself with the people he could manipulate to keep his personal agenda moving forward.

Using your tools of observation, how is it that the department that should be exhibiting diversity had none? Gary has either fired or pushed out anyone who wasn't helping him achieve his agenda. Even the director of the HR department was caught in his agenda. It's a shame, but personal agendas can affect a company overall. In 2014, this same company paid out a lawsuit to several people who claimed they were discriminated against in promotion or lateral job changes. His personal agenda spread and cost the company $2.5 million to four employees who documented what happened to them. This company was ranked in top 100 places to work in Georgia, and today they are just a place to work.

Personal agendas are destructive.

Story Time: I had an assistant manager who was a superstar; there was no doubt he had the drive and ability to do great things.

I groomed him, trained him, positioned him to get noticed for his great work. Come to find out he was plotting to get me fired by telling everyone that I was coming to work late every day and leaving early every day. Well, documentation will save your life. I was a salaried manager who used the timeclock to clock in and out because I will never allow anyone to question how much I'm working and when I come to work and leave work. So, after getting him promoted to his own store, his personal agenda kept going: He was still trying to get other store managers fired, so he would be the most experienced and knowledgeable in the area. I even sat down with this Gary at lunch one day and told him, "If you continue to crush others just to move up the ladder, when the day comes you get crushed you will fall so far and so hard." Needless to say, a few months later, I was terminated, and it was because I hadn't moved the needle. I'm not going to say I was the best manager ever for this company, but later I learned that he began talking about me with the district manager. He would set up conversations with me and then report back to the boss about what was said or what I did. When I was terminated, I went to our HQ with a blue binder of everything I had documented in my store. Good, bad, and indifferent. After two weeks, I was rehired, placed back in my old role, and got a $6,000 raise, which I'm sure was to keep me from making a bigger issue. About a month after I returned, I was offered a position of greater responsibility, greater territory, and greater possibilities from a new company. I left, and the company gave me a new role six miles from my house and a Monday-through-Friday schedule—and no more agendas poisoning my work. After I left, about two years later, I ran into Gary and said, "Hey, I know what you did to get me fired. I just need you to know that I know what you did." By the way, he was promoted twice in the company—and then he fell, as I predicted. He was accused of sexual harassment three times; after the third, he was terminated. His agenda expanded because he felt untouchable and protected by those around him. His luck ran out, and he is no longer a landscape manager.

Personal agendas can also be positive and helpful. Many times, as a leader, if you have a management staff that has an aligned agenda personally and professionally, your job and their job can go smooth and easy. To this day, I can name managers and leaders who worked with me and for me that I stay in touch with because, together, we did great things. Their agendas lined up with mine and that of the companies. The residual effect of this alignment as well is in today's work force. You can expect an employee to work for more companies in his/her career. The leaders you hire have people they trust that they will bring with them. I did it as a regional manager, district manager, and even an owner. The company I currently work for just hired a new president—and who does he bring in? His old army buddy as VP of operations. When you have a personal agenda that aligns with that of others as well as the company's agenda, you will not only build an outstanding professional network but will not have trouble getting hired or learning about new opportunities.

How can you draw out agendas? One word: INTERACTION. If you continue to interact with your peers, your staff, and your boss, you can use your tools. Some of the best cues I have seen or heard and picked up on are as follows. EMOTIONAL INTELLIGENCE. This is a great indicator of an agenda. Emotional intelligence indicates how one react and communicates via emotion. I'm not talking about passion. Emotion is when it becomes blame-shifting. It becomes gossip. It becomes smart-ass comments about a person or a policy or decision. That is emotional intelligence; in those negative cases, your radar should blip, and you should start to inquire the reason behind the lack of emotional intelligence.

Second, and I use this one a lot: If you're not offering solutions, then all you are doing is whining. Whining is a sign of not knowing or not caring, so you are trying to misdirect away from you. Why do that? What is your agenda that makes you behave this way? Start inquiring. Listen to them, though. We don't make assumptions until we have done our due diligence. Third, when assigning tasks, gauge the reaction of your assignment. Sometimes it's not what I asked you to do it's how you reacted to it when I asked you. Maybe they feel that is below their pay grade or responsibility; maybe it's not in their job requirements. Inquire as to why that happened.

Fourth: Disrespecting the chain of command. This one is easy. If you are truly holding yourself accountable, then you should not have any issues with the chain of command. Information should flow freely up and down the chain. If you have team members or staff jumping over someone in the chain; then, that is disrespectful and needs to be discussed. Maybe they are not getting the response they need, and they move it up the chain, but they should hold themselves accountable as well and give you the facts and why the decision was made to skip a person in the chain. All four of these incidents are behavioral and directly show you the attitude of that individual. Do not let these go without investigation. Do not let any of these or any other incidents or behaviors go without discussion or inquiry. The four I listed aren't everything. You need to raise your situational awareness and perceptions of your environment and tune in to the pulse of the people around you as well as those you lead. Trust your gut; trust your intuition. Take action; be a leader.

Now go on the offense. Bring the agenda into the light. The last thing one wants is his/her agenda to be exposed and be public. Announce it to the world in a team meeting. You don't directly call them out, but you can look them dead in the eye and ask, "What do you want?" In front of their peers, they will crumble because they won't admit to their agenda; they will stumble and not know what to say. Then, address it directly but privately. Now you have the team or department aware that you can address it with the individual and get everything out in the open. Make that individual answer to his/

her actions. Finally, assign tasks and duties to the person based on the company's agenda—not his or hers. Make sure that person has clear concise instructions with deadlines. If he/she wants to have an agenda, then that person will learn to align with company agenda or not enjoy work life. That person will decide what he/she wants to do, but it will not be at the expense of the team or you and your job. Overall, ask questions. If you don't know what question to ask, then just ask why. Observe that person's actions. ACTION IS THE ONLY TRUTH. Do his/her words match the actions?

Again, there is so much more to this than what is presented in this chapter. But this is a great overall start and will certainly open up the playing field and help you be a better leader and root out the negative and move in a positive profitable direction. Remember, if you truly believe what's right is right then prove it and let that person's agenda fail. If you do the right thing at the right time for the right reasons, you still may not win and will possibly get disciplined or even lose your job. But at least you can put your head on your pillow at night and say, "I stood up for the right reasons."

This call to action is difficult. As discussed, sometimes doing the right thing can get you in between a rock and a hard place. The wounds of honor are always self-inflicted. You must remember that it's your livelihood and your earnings that you put at risk when you stand up for what is right. It's honorable but so is providing for your family. If you are ready and prepared for that road, then more power to you to go down it. I have done it. It worked out okay. I have done it, and it got me fired. You must be prepared to deal with the choices and the actions you take when standing up for what is right. Keep in mind that what is right is what you think and know is right. What happens if the facts change and or the landscape changes? Then what? Honor and respect are earned. When you stand up for what is right, it's because you've earned the privilege to do so. But are you willing to sacrifice yourself to make that stand?

CHAPTER 6

Human Beings Are the Weirdest Creatures on Earth

This chapter is about the unimaginable task of trying to figure out human beings. It doesn't matter how many books you've read or how many degrees or MBAs you have—you will never figure out human beings. We are the weirdest creatures on Earth. One day, we are fine. The next day we hate you and everyone around you. No two of us are the same, think the same, feel the same, react the same. As a leader, how in the hell do you lead when you can't figure them out fully? That's why you get paid the wage you do. It's to put you in the position to figure out the best way to manage human beings as possible, which seems impossible the majority of the time . Every chapter in this book talks about using this skill or this tool in your tool box to help you lead and motivate those you lead and manage. So, then, what is this chapter about? It's about having the self-awareness that we all have quirks, bad days, good days, weird mannerisms. The greatest tool you have as a leader is to be human. No one is perfect. I am far from perfect. But I am human. I try my best to understand human beings and why they do what they do.

Story Time: When I was a consultant, I had a client who was a mechanic shop, and one of his techs told me to never say "good morning" to him because he hates mornings. My response was, "Okay, there is nothing wrong with saying good morning, so I will continue to say 'good morning' whether he liked it or not. If 'good morning' is the one thing that ruins your day, well then too bad." To me and most of regular society, this behavior is weird. It is also a sign of "You're not going to tell me what to do." I do what I want, when I want, and how I want to do it. Thus, every day I was on site with this client, I said hello and good morning to everyone— including him. So, after six weeks on site, I approached him, and he said "good morning" to me first. Why? Why the change in behavior? Only he knows. But the fact is that I treated him like a human. Yes, I said "good morning," even though he didn't like it, but I just treated him like I treat everyone else—no better, no worse. So why did it work on him? Why didn't it work on someone else in a similar situation? You will never know, and you will never figure it out.

Yes. You can earn a degree studying human beings and their mannerisms, tendencies, routines. How does this translate to everyday business and leadership? Be human, I guess. Hell, I don't know. Does anyone? One of the best techniques I use to get me on the right road when dealing with human beings is to ask them what they want. Don't let them give you a predictable answer like "I want more money." We all want more money! We all want those things in our lives that are needs. WHAT DO YOU WANT? I MEAN TRULY WANT? "Well, I really really really want money!" But you need to define the difference of a want and a need with this one simple exercise: List all of the things they tell you they want. Then say, "Okay. Are you willing to fight for this want?" This will prioritize their mindset but also help you as a leader get into the mind of your people. What makes them happy, sad, angry, lazy, tired? What are their pet peeves? How do they react and adapt to your leadership style? How can you help them to achieve their wants? How can we work together to achieve the wants? If they aren't willing to fight for their wants, then they aren't true wants. Again, we are trying to understand a human being who, in two weeks, will be a different person. People change—but not drastically, unless a drastic event happens in their lives. I always lead and managed my people and teams with the understanding that you are who you are and that is why you are on my team.

I'm not talking about having a bad day or not feeling well and not being yourself. I'm talking about spending 40+ hours a week with people and understanding them and their behaviors. Trying to understand the *why* to the things they do. Why do you like sugar in your coffee? Why do you hate the color red? Those are the details that will make your life and leadership so much easier. Building a team of completely different personalities is the hardest job in the world, next to being single mother. Managing and leading human beings with different wants and desires can only be done if you understand them and can put them all together like a puzzle, so they fit as a cohesive unit that benefits the common goal and/or agenda. If you look at those who are successful at what they do in the business world, they may have simply maintained a high level of functionality in the human being. You can't figure them out, but you can at least do the best to maximize the wants of the people. Ever since we were young, when we get what we want we are happy. How many times on Linked-in or Facebook have you read that happy employees do better work or higher-quality work? So, not to bring you down from having a great team and making them happy, but how do you keep a team happy without sacrificing your leadership role? How do you maintain it without losing authority? I've had a saying for a long time: Just when everything seems to be working the way you want it to and expect it to, it will go sideways in the next few days. Then, we are starting all over. New wants, new needs, new agendas, maybe new people, maybe a new boss or leader.

You will die a miserable death if you try to figure it out. Worry about what you can control; the rest is just someone else's stress. You choose to absorb it or deal with it.

Why do we associate with people we have never met, but we claim them to be friends because they are fans of the same sports team we cheer for or the same band we listen to? If we really knew any of these people outside of our common interests, I promise you that 95% of those people we wouldn't want to associate with. How many of your friends on Facebook do you even know? How many have you met and had a meaningful conversation with? I have 625 friends on Facebook, and I would say that, on the high side, 10% of them I actually know and or have an acquaintance with. Yes, I have chatted with them or done business with them, but, if they were in a line up, I couldn't pick them out of anyone else. How is that the new definition of friends?

This is the Sales Class 101: The first thing is to find the association with your potential customer. We all have that passion or button that, if you push it, we are either your best friend or your fiercest enemy. We read all the time about first impressions; that, when you introduce yourself, the other person is formulating an opinion in the first 15 to 30 seconds. Why? We have barely said "hello," but because of the way this person wears his/her hair, clothing, shoes, glasses, maybe the way this person carries him/herself, we have already formed an opinion of whether or we like this person. That's absolutely crazy. I'm not judging. We all I do it. I do it; you do it. That is why human beings are the weirdest creatures on Earth.

Look at the interview process. We do out best to pull the mask off of the interviewee because we know he/she is putting on a show and that we will see who this person truly is in a few months after being hired. Look at dating apps: You swipe left or right in a matter of seconds. You haven't even met them to see if they are a personality match or not, we just *swipe swipe swipe*. Crazy that we can't communicate with someone and get to know them and their personality before we make an assessment about them. Look at your neighborhood. When I was a kid, we had block parties. We all knew each other; we knew each other's kids, jobs, schedules. Nowadays, all we do is wave and say hi. Texting and instant messaging have disconnected us from communicating with each other; yet, we continue to make judgments of others.

What the hell does this have to do with being a grown ass leader? Think about this: How effective can you be when you are more self-aware? When you can ask the right questions? When you can understand more than just surface reactions? How equipped as a leader are you when you can probe and position an employee or staffer to help push those buttons and make the connection to maximize his/her performance? Of course, until they adapt and change because they will adapt and change. I don't have a lot of friends, but I will tell you that everyone who has ever met me thought I was a complete asshole when we first met. But, once they spent time with me, interacted with me, they found out that I was caring, with wired sense of humor, a lover of horror films, sports memorabilia, and cats. Even my wife of 22 years hated my guts when she first met me, but now, we have been together 25 years and married 22. That doesn't work if we continue to be the weirdest creatures on Earth. As a leader, you must know that fact. You must know how you can get a group of weirdos to work as a unit or department or a team.

Think about this, too: How many people have you managed or led, and they ended up getting fired for something stupid life theft or sexual harassment. What happened? I'm sure they were a great employee, but you never saw that coming. Something changed them from that new employee who wanted to succeed and do great things to the employee who didn't care about the consequences of his/her actions. Be a leader and engage your people—not to the point of being nosey. It's okay to ask questions and keep asking questions to make sure you put forth the effort. We are creatures of routing, so when you notice the routing change or something's out of sync, you engage and do your best to get them to talk to you. You are not their psychiatrist. You are not qualified to treat them, but you are qualified to listen—and a lot of times that is enough.

For the final chapter call to action, here is one of the greatest things you can do: Observe people—everywhere, i.e., in the grocery store, airport, doctor's office. Just like watching animals in their natural environment, you need to observe humans in their natural environment. Your call to action, then, is to be observant and listen anywhere you see human interaction. This has certainly helped me to better understand human nature. I'm no expert, but you can become an astute observer to human behavior and emotions, which is a skill that will help you immensely in your career.

CHAPTER 7

Closing

How do I wrap this up in a pretty bow? That's not my style nor will I do that. This book is not the know-all end-all. This is not the bible for you to follow and quote blindly. This is just one guy's experience, a guy who has failed and failed miserably. He has witnessed failure of others, the success of others, and his own success. It's normal to have these experiences. Here, I simply want to shine a light on behaviors and techniques that I have used that work amazingly. I'm not a CEO. I'm not a VP or some power player who books giant speaking engagements and is seen as an expert. I'm just a leader who has learned over the years what make the best leader. You aren't perfect; neither am I. Focus on the things that you can control and should control. Focus your energy, even if it's just on one of the things in this book, and you can be a better leader/manager/owner. Remember to be genuine and be yourself. Remember that nobody is perfect, and nobody ever will be. I see a ton of managers/leaders/owners who continue to struggle and have no clue what to do. They panic and revert to working in their business instead of on it. This will hopefully assist you and your people to be more productive and understanding of the landscape of people in business.

Remember you are who you are—until you make yourself better. Being better means being on time, being accountable, being a great listener, being one thing better than you were yesterday. The idea is that there is no better thing on Earth than to successfully interact with others. I hope this book helps you to learn something. Just one thing.

I want to also thank everyone who every worked for me and every manager, supervisor, and leader I worked for. Because your behaviors helped me create this philosophy. To all of my clients I have consulted, I hope this helps maintain the message. Finally, to all of my pro-athlete friends who, when I was putting this together, kept saying "be a grown ass man and make a grown ass decision." Thank you for the inspiration. I am truly grateful for all of those above for making this possible.

Made in the USA
Lexington, KY
06 December 2019